AS YOU LIKE IT

NOTES

including
- *Life of Shakespeare*
- *Brief Synopsis of the Play*
- *List of Characters*
- *Summaries and Commentaries*
- *Character Analyses*
- *Critical Analysis*
- *Questions for Review*
- *Selected Bibliography*

by
Tom Smith, M.A.
Department of Theater
State University of New Mexico

Cliffs Notes

INCORPORATED

LINCOLN, NEBRASKA 68501

Editor

Gary Carey, M.A.
University of Colorado

Consulting Editor

James L. Roberts, Ph.D.
Department of English
University of Nebraska

ISBN 0-8220-0007-5
© Copyright 1981
by
C. K. Hillegass
All Rights Reserved
Printed in U.S.A.

1993 Printing

Cliffs Notes, Inc.   Lincoln, Nebraska

CONTENTS

AS YOU LIKE IT NOTES

LIFE OF SHAKESPEARE

Many books have assembled facts, reasonable suppositions, traditions, and speculations concerning the life and career of William Shakespeare. Taken as a whole, these materials give a rather comprehensive picture of England's foremost dramatic poet. Tradition and sober supposition are not necessarily false because they lack proved bases for their existence. It is important, however, that persons interested in Shakespeare should distinguish between *facts* and *beliefs* about his life.

From one point of view, modern scholars are fortunate to know as much as they do about a man of middle-class origin who left a small English country town and embarked on a professional career in sixteenth-century London. From another point of view, they know surprisingly little about the writer who has continued to influence the English language and its drama and poetry for more than three hundred years. Sparse and scattered as these facts of his life are, they are sufficient to prove that a man from Stratford by the name of William Shakespeare wrote the major portion of the thirty-seven plays which scholars ascribe to him. The concise review which follows will concern itself with some of these records.

No one knows the exact date of William Shakespeare's birth. His baptism occurred on Wednesday, April 26, 1564. His father was John Shakespeare, tanner, glover, dealer in grain, and town official of Stratford; his mother, Mary, was the daughter of Robert Arden, a prosperous gentleman-farmer. The Shakespeares lived on Henley Street.

Under a bond dated November 28, 1582, William Shakespeare and Anne Hathaway entered into a marriage contract. The baptism of their eldest child, Susanna, took place in Stratford in May, 1583. One year and nine months later their twins, Hamnet and Judith, were christened in the same church. The parents named them for the poet's friends Hamnet and Judith Sadler.

Early in 1596, William Shakespeare, in his father's name, applied to the College of Heralds for a coat of arms. Although positive proof is lacking, there is reason to believe that the Heralds granted this request, for in 1599 Shakespeare again made application for the right to quarter his coat of arms with that of his mother. Entitled to her father's coat of arms, Mary had lost this privilege when she married John Shakespeare before he held the official status of gentleman.

In May of 1597, Shakespeare purchased New Place, the outstanding residential property in Stratford at that time. Since John Shakespeare had suffered financial reverses prior to this date, William must have achieved success for himself.

Court records show that in 1601 or 1602, William Shakespeare began rooming in the household of Christopher Mountjoy in London. Subsequent disputes between Shakespeare's landlord, Mountjoy, and his son-in-law, Stephen Belott, over Stephen's wedding settlement led to a series of legal actions, and in 1612 the court scribe recorded Shakespeare's deposition of testimony relating to the case.

In July, 1605, William Shakespeare paid four hundred and forty pounds for the lease of a large portion of the tithes on certain real estate in and near Stratford. This was an arrangement whereby Shakespeare purchased half the annual tithes, or taxes, on certain agricultural products from sections of land in and near Stratford. In addition to receiving approximately ten percent income on his investment, he almost doubled his capital. This was possibly the most important and successful investment of his lifetime, and it paid a steady income for many years.

Shakespeare is next mentioned when John Combe, a resident of Stratford, died on July 12, 1614. To his friend, Combe bequeathed the sum of five pounds. These records and similar ones are important, not because of their economic significance but because they prove the existence of a William Shakespeare in Stratford and in London during this period.

On March 25, 1616, William Shakespeare revised his last will and testament. He died on April 23 of the same year. His body lies within the chancel and before the altar of the Stratford church. A rather wry inscription is carved upon his tombstone:

Good Friend, for Jesus' sake, forbear
To dig the dust enclosed here;
Blest be the man that spares these stones
And curst be he that moves my bones.

The last direct descendant of William Shakespeare was his grand-daughter, Elizabeth Hall, who died in 1670.

These are the most outstanding facts about Shakespeare the man, as apart from those about the dramatist and poet. Such pieces of information, scattered from 1564 through 1616, declare the existence of such a person, not as a writer or actor, but as a private citizen. It is illogical to think that anyone would or could have fabricated these details for the purpose of deceiving later generations.

In similar fashion, the evidence establishing William Shakespeare as the foremost playwright of his day is positive and persuasive. Robert Greene's *Groatsworth of Wit*, in which he attacked Shakespeare, a mere actor, for presuming to write plays in competition with Greene and his fellow playwrights, was entered in the *Stationers' Register* on September 20, 1592. In 1594 Shakespeare acted before Queen Elizabeth, and in 1594 and 1595 his name appeared as one of the shareholders of the Lord Chamberlain's Company. Francis Meres in his *Palladis Tamia* (1598) called Shakespeare "mellifluous and hony-tongued" and compared his comedies and tragedies with those of Plautus and Seneca in excellence.

Shakespeare's continued association with Burbage's company is equally definite. His name appears as one of the owners of the Globe in 1599. On May 19, 1603, he and his fellow actors received a patent from James I designating them as the King's Men and making them Grooms of the Chamber. Late in 1608 or early in 1609, Shakespeare and his colleagues purchased the Blackfriars Theatre and began using it as their winter location when weather made production at the Globe inconvenient.

Other specific allusions to Shakespeare, to his acting and his writing, occur in numerous places. Put together, they form irrefutable testimony that William Shakespeare of Stratford and London was the leader among Elizabethan playwrights.

One of the most impressive of all proofs of Shakespeare's authorship of his plays is the First Folio of 1623, with the dedicatory verse which appeared in it. John Heminge and Henry Condell, members of Shakespeare's own company, stated that they collected and issued the plays as a memorial to their fellow actor. Many contemporary poets contributed eulogies to Shakespeare; one of the best known of these poems is by Ben Jonson, a fellow actor and later, a friendly rival. Jonson also criticized Shakespeare's dramatic work in *Timber: or, Discoveries* (1641).

Certainly there are many things about Shakespeare's genius and career which the most diligent scholars do not know and cannot explain, but the facts which do exist are sufficient to establish Shakespeare's identity as a man and his authorship of the thirty-seven plays which reputable critics acknowledge to be his.

BRIEF SYNOPSIS OF THE PLAY

Orlando, the youngest son of the now deceased Sir Roland de Boys, complains to Adam, the old family retainer, that his eldest brother, Oliver, has kept his inheritance from him—that is, Oliver has neglected training Orlando to be a proper gentleman. Oliver arrives on the scene, and a bitter quarrel takes place. Adam parts the fighting brothers, and Oliver coldly promises to give Orlando his due. Learning that Orlando intends to challenge Duke Frederick's champion wrestler, a brute of a man called Charles, Oliver makes plans to have his brother killed in the ring. He convinces the slow-witted Charles that Orlando is plotting against him and that Orlando should be killed.

At the match the next day, Duke Frederick, his daughter Celia, and his niece, Rosalind, watch Charles and Orlando wrestle. Charles has seriously injured his first three opponents, but in the match with Orlando, the young man's great speed and agility defeat the duke's champion. At first, Frederick is very cordial to Orlando, but when he learns the youth's identity, he becomes furious and leaves. The reason for this is that Orlando's dead father, Sir Roland de Boys, had at one time been Frederick's bitter enemy.

After Frederick stalks out, Celia and Rosalind congratulate Orlando, and Rosalind makes it clear that she finds him most attractive. Orlando returns her feelings, but he is so tongue-tied with embarrassment that he can say nothing.

At the ducal palace, we discover that Celia and her cousin Rosalind are as close as sisters; Rosalind is the daughter of the rightful duke, Duke Senior, whose throne has been usurped by his brother, Frederick. Frederick has banished Duke Senior, along with a band of his faithful followers, to the Forest of Arden to live the life of simple foresters. Until now, it is only the strong bond between Rosalind and Celia that prevents Duke Frederick from sending Rosalind away to share her father's exile. But suddenly, Frederick storms into the palace, accuses Rosalind of plotting against him, and despite Celia's pleas for her cousin, he banishes Rosalind. After her father leaves, Celia decides to go into exile with her cousin, and the girls set out for the Forest of Arden—Rosalind disguised as a young man, "Ganymede," and Celia disguised as a young country lass, "Aliena." Touchstone, Frederick's jester, accompanies them.

Meanwhile, Orlando returns home and is warned by the faithful Adam that Oliver is plotting to kill him. Together, they too decide to set out for the Forest of Arden, hoping that they will find safety there.

When his daughter Celia is missed, Frederick sends his men out to find Orlando. When he is informed of Orlando's flight to the Forest of Arden, Frederick assumes that Orlando is responsible for Celia's disappearance, and in a rage he sends for Oliver and commands him to find Orlando or else forfeit his entire estate to Frederick.

In the forest, Orlando and Adam join Rosalind's exiled father and his men, while Rosalind and Celia, still in disguise, purchase a little cottage and a small herd of sheep and settle down to a peaceful, pastoral existence. One day, however, Rosalind finds that the trees in the forest are all covered with sheets of poetry, dedicated to her. The author of these poems, of course, is Orlando. So, still pretending to be the young man Ganymede, Rosalind meets Orlando, who is in the throes of love-sickness for having apparently lost Rosalind. Ganymede offers to cure Orlando of his love-sickness by pretending to be his lady-love, Rosalind. Orlando, she says, should woo Ganymede as though "he" were Rosalind. In turn, Ganymede will do "his best" to act as moody and capricious as a girl might just do and, eventually, Orlando will weary of all the coy teasing and forget all about love—and Rosalind. Orlando agrees to try the plan.

Rosalind, meanwhile, continues to assume the guise of Ganymede and becomes accidentally involved in yet another complication: Silvius, a young shepherd, falls in love with Phebe, a hardhearted shepherdess, but Phebe rejects Silvius's attentions and falls in love with the young, good-looking Ganymede.

In the midst of all this confusion, Oliver arrives in the Forest of Arden. He tells Ganymede of a near escape he has just had with death. His brother, Orlando, he says, saved him from being poisoned by a deadly snake as he slept, and later, Orlando killed a lioness which was ready to pounce on Oliver. Oliver then tells Ganymede that he has been sent to this part of the forest to seek out a young man known as Ganymede and tell him that Orlando cannot keep his appointment with him. And there is more news: while saving Oliver's life, Orlando was wounded. Hearing this, Ganymede swoons.

Later, in another part of the forest, Oliver and Celia meet and fall in love at first sight, and the jester, Touchstone, falls in love with a homely, simple-minded young woman named Audrey, who tends a herd of goats. Touchstone chases off Audrey's suitor, a lout named William, and although he realizes that he will never instill in Audrey any understanding of, or love for, such things as poetry, he still feels that he must have her.

Duke Frederick, meanwhile, is alarmed by the daily exodus of so many of the best men of his court to the alliance which is growing in the Forest of Arden; he therefore decides to journey to the forest himself and put a stop to all this business. At the forest's edge, however, he meets an old religious hermit and is miraculously converted.

At this point, Rosalind, still disguised as Ganymede, promises to solve the problems of everyone by magic. Shedding her male attire in private, she suddenly appears as herself, and the play comes to a swift close as she and Orlando, Oliver and Celia, and Silvius and Phebe are married. Rosalind's father, the rightful duke, is joyous at finding his daughter again and is returned to his ducal status. Frederick's conversion is so complete that he renounces the world. At the end of the play, Rosalind comes forward and addresses the audience in a short but charming epilogue. In particular, she talks to all the lovers in the audience and wishes them well.

LIST OF CHARACTERS

Orlando de Boys

This young Englishman is noble and pure of heart. His constant concern and care for Adam, the old family servant, immediately makes the audience esteem him. When he learns that his brother Oliver is planning to kill him, he leaves home and goes to the Forest of Arden with old Adam. In the forest, he attaches love poems addressed to Rosalind all over the trees. Finally, he and Rosalind are united and wed.

Oliver de Boys

He is supposed to teach his younger brother Orlando to be a gentleman, but he does not do so; he is a treacherous youth and tries to have Orlando killed. Orlando, however, saves him from being killed by a deadly snake and, later, from a fierce lioness and, finally the two brothers are reconciled. Oliver eventually falls in love with Celia.

Jaques de Boys

Like Oliver and Orlando, he is one of the sons of the late Sir Roland de Boys. He is favored by Oliver over Orlando, and he is sent away to school to learn how to be a proper gentleman. At the end of the play, he appears onstage and announces that the corrupt Duke Frederick has been converted to a life of goodness by an old hermit.

Duke Frederick

The "villain" of this comedy, he banishes his elder brother and eventually he also exiles his brother's daughter, Rosalind, from the ducal palace. Just before the play ends, he is converted by a religious hermit and, henceforward, he chooses to lead a monastic life in the Forest of Arden.

Rosalind

She is the most realistic and sympathetic character in the play. She falls in love with Orlando and shortly thereafter, she is exiled from the ducal court by Frederick. Accompanied by Celia and Touchstone, she goes to the Forest of Arden disguised as a young man, Ganymede. In the forest, she is wooed by Orlando, who is unaware that she is, in reality, his beloved Rosalind.

Celia

She is Rosalind's cousin and closest friend. When Rosalind is exiled by Celia's father, Celia accompanies Rosalind to the Forest of Arden. Since Celia isn't in love at the time, her practical answers to Rosalind's queries about love help to explore the depth of Rosalind's love for Orlando. Celia goes to the forest disguised as Aliena. Eventually she meets Orlando's brother Oliver and falls in love with him.

Touchstone

The court clown, he accompanies Rosalind and Celia to the Forest of Arden. There he falls in love with Audrey, a country woman. Touchstone is one of Shakespeare's greatest "fools." Yet he is very realistic in his philosophy, and he serves as a norm by which we can view the other characters.

Jaques

He is a man of the world, a free spirit. In his travels, he has affected Continental mannerisms of speech and dress, and he believes that his ideas are terribly profound when actually they are very shallow and very generalized. Jaques is satirized by almost everyone with whom he holds "deep discussions."

Duke Senior

His ducal rights are usurped, and he is banished to the Forest of Arden by his younger brother, Frederick. Ultimately, his lands and his possessions are returned to him.

Adam

He is the de Boys' old family retainer. He is dismissed by the nasty Oliver, and later he relates to Orlando that Oliver plans to kill Orlando while he sleeps. He accompanies Orlando to the Forest of Arden.

Corin

In contrast to Silvius, Corin is a real shepherd; he is quite knowledgeable about sheep and their care. His lines serve as a contrast to the courtly wit of Touchstone. He also serves as a contrast to the pastoral lovers, Silvius and Phebe.

Audrey

This simple country woman, along with William and Corin, serves as a contrast to the "town" characters. She has trouble expressing her thoughts and cannot fathom the wit of Touchstone, but their love is so rapturous that eventually they are wed.

Silvius

This shepherd represents the romantic lover in the pastoral genre of Elizabethan literature. He loves the shepherdess Phebe, but she constantly rejects him; despite this fact, however, he pines for her throughout the play and constantly threatens suicide if his love remains unrequited. Unlike Corin, he knows absolutely nothing about sheep.

Phebe

As the pastoral girl who is the beloved of Silvius, she is a stock figure of this type of romance—that is, she rejects the advances of Silvius, while he suffers from the woes of love-sickness. Surprisingly, she falls wildly in love with Ganymede (Rosalind in disguise), yet finally she weds Silvius.

William

He is a stock country character who serves as a contrast to the pastoral lovers, Silvius and Phebe, and also as a contrast to the "town characters."

Amiens

A lord attending Duke Senior; he has a light, delightful role and in this role, he sings some of the most beautiful lyrics that Shakespeare ever wrote.

Le Beau

He represents the man-about-town. He speaks well but knows little, and his speech, his dress, and his mannerisms are all satirized in the play.

Charles

A professional wrestler whom Oliver tells to kill—or at least, maim—Orlando. Ironically, Orlando wins the match.

Sir Oliver Martext

This vicar is not too knowledgeable; he almost joins Touchstone and Audrey in wedlock, but Touchstone is dissuaded at the last moment by Jaques.

Hymen

The god of marriage appears in the final scene of the play to lead the masque and to give dignity to the subsequent marriage ceremony.

Dennis

Servant to Oliver de Boys.

SUMMARIES AND COMMENTARIES

ACT I – SCENE 1

Summary

In the orchard of the house of Oliver de Boys, Orlando de Boys complains to Adam, an old family servant, about how he has been treated by his elder brother, Oliver, who, according to their father's will, was to see to it that Orlando was to be taught all the ways of being a gentleman, as Oliver has been doing for their brother Jaques. Yet Orlando has been kept at home, like a peasant. Oliver enters and Orlando tells him that "the spirit of my father, which I think is within me, begins to mutiny against this servitude." The two brothers argue, and suddenly Orlando grabs Oliver and demands that either he receive the education and the treatment due him or else he wants the thousand crowns which he is entitled to, according to their father's will. Oliver dismisses him with a curt "Well, sir, get you in. I will not long be troubled with you; you shall have some part of your will." Turning to Adam, he insultingly sneers, "Get you with him, you old dog."

Orlando and Adam leave, and Oliver's anger is interrupted when his servant, Dennis, enters with the news that Charles, the duke's wrestler, is at the door. Oliver summons the wrestler, and the two of them discuss news of the court. The old duke has been banished by his younger brother and has gone into exile in the Forest of Arden and has been joined by some of his loyal lords, where they "live like the old Robin Hood of England . . . and fleet the time carelessly, as they did in the golden world." The old duke's daughter, Rosalind, however, has remained at court with her inseparable companion, Celia, the usurper's daughter.

Charles then says that the new duke has announced that wrestling matches will be held at court the next day. Moreover, Charles has heard that Orlando intends to come in disguise and "try a fall" with him. He warns Oliver that, although he does not want to do harm to Orlando, he would be required to best him for his own honor. Oliver assures Charles that he need not be concerned. "I had as lief thou didst break his neck as his finger," he says, and adds that Orlando is dangerous and will kill Charles by "some treacherous device" if he survives the bout. Charles agrees, therefore, to take care of Orlando and leaves. Alone, Oliver says of Orlando, "I hope I shall see an end of him; for my soul—yet I know not why—hates nothing more than he." Anticipating the match the next day, he goes off to "kindle" Orlando for the match.

Commentary

This first scene establishes several conflicts. The two major conflicts are between the two pairs of brothers: Oliver and Orlando, and between Duke Frederick and Duke Senior. In each case, a brother is wronged, and he is wronged for the same reason—that is, he is wronged because he is well-liked and morally good. It is interesting to note that in the case of Duke Frederick and Duke Senior, it is the *younger* brother who is usurping the rights of the *elder* brother, whereas with Oliver and Orlando it is just the opposite. In his dialogue with Oliver, Orlando explains the villainy of Duke Frederick: it is the right of the first-born male child to inherit his father's properties. Therefore, when Duke Frederick usurped the dukedom from his *elder* brother, he committed an unnatural act, according to the mores of the Elizabethan era.

Oliver's own villainy is explained in Orlando's opening speech, in which he relates Oliver's failure to execute their father's will. Clearly, both Duke Frederick and Oliver violate the natural laws of ascendancy. Oliver's villainy is even further evident when he coldly and abruptly tells Adam, the old and faithful family servant, to leave the room. But Oliver's cruel nature is made absolutely clear when he *lies* to Charles, a professional wrestler, and encourages him to at least maim, if he cannot kill, Orlando. Thus the laws governing the family are being horribly violated. Biblically, fratricide is the oldest crime of all.

These unnatural acts between brothers contrast sharply with the idyllic ambience in the Forest of Arden, where the main action of the play is about to occur. Already we are being prepared for these pastoral elements of the play; for example, consider the setting of Scene 1, which is set in Oliver's orchard. Although the setting is reflective of the pastoral life, it is also a part of the "real" world in which brother is pitted against brother. Eventually, it is to the Forest of Arden, a fantasy world, that the characters will flee to sort out their problems and their loves.

Scene 1 also focuses on the matter of city life versus country living, a question much in discussion in Elizabethan England and much in vogue recently. Orlando first gives voice to this question in his opening speech, when he points out that he is being kept ". . . rustically at home . . ." without the benefit of being sent away to study gentlemanly ways. Later, he decides to leave his pastoral home to seek his fortune elsewhere. This question of sophisticated city living versus the simplicity of a pastoral life runs throughout the play. It is treated in a general and slightly humorous way by

Jaques in his famous "All the world's a stage . . ." speech (Act II, Scene 7) and hilariously in the confrontation between Touchstone, the country fool, and Corin, the country shepherd (Act III, Scene 2). Yet despite the question's being considered throughout the play, it is never answered satisfactorily.

In addition to the natural versus the unnatural, and city life versus country life, Shakespeare also uses the formalities of his language to establish the various social levels of his characters. For example, when Oliver first addresses Charles, he uses the formal pronoun *you*, but when he cunningly seeks to dupe Charles into killing Orlando, he uses the familiar pronoun *thou*. In other words, by his use of pronouns, Shakespeare indicates that Oliver has become condescending towards Charles. This device is used frequently throughout the play.

ACT I–SCENE 2

Summary

Celia, the daughter of Duke Frederick, and Rosalind, the daughter of the deposed duke, are talking on the lawn before the duke's palace. Celia chides Rosalind for not being sufficiently "merry," and Rosalind, although she grieves because of her father's exile, promises to try and be cheerful and "devise sports." Touchstone, the court clown, enters, joins in their repartee, and tells Celia that Frederick has summoned her. They are joined by Le Beau, a courtier, who brings news of a wrestling contest which is to begin shortly on the lawn. Charles has already beaten three challengers, breaking their ribs and very nearly killing them.

Duke Frederick, Charles, Orlando, and members of the court arrive, and Frederick suggests that the young women try to dissuade the challenger from the contest as he will surely be injured. They try to do so, but Orlando will not be convinced, saying, "I shall do my friends no wrong, for I have none to lament me; the world no injury, for in it I have nothing." To everyone's surprise, Orlando wins the fall and wishes to try a second, but Charles has to be carried out. Frederick asks to know Orlando's name and becomes furious when he discovers that Orlando is the son of Roland de Boys, an old enemy. "Thou shouldst have better pleased me with this deed,/ Hadst thou descended from another house," he says.

Celia, Rosalind, and Orlando are left alone on the lawn, and Rosalind, whose father loved Orlando "as his soul," gives Orlando her necklace to wear as a reward for his gallantry. They are instantly attracted to each other, and, symbolically, Orlando is "overthrown" by Rosalind—in spite of the fact that he was not overthrown by Charles. As the women leave, Le Beau rushes in to warn Orlando that the duke is angry; he counsels him to leave immediately. Orlando also learns that the duke has lately "ta'en displeasure 'gainst his gentle niece," Rosalind, because the people praise and pity her. He decides to return home, to leave a "tyrant duke" and face a "tyrant brother."

Commentary

This scene further reveals the pains and problems of the "real" world. (Later, however, in the idyllic fantasy of the Forest of Arden, Jaques is troubled when he discovers the carcass of a deer, his "velvet friend," in Act II, Scene 1.) In this real world, Shakespeare introduces and contrasts the theme of love. There is, for example, the love between Celia and Rosalind (the word *love* also had the connotation of friendship to the Elizabethans). Their love is pure and innocent, especially when contrasted to the complete lack of feeling between the two pairs of brothers. In a witty dialogue, Rosalind and Celia discuss the merits of love as a sport where one can fall in love and have the "safety of a pure blush . . . in honour." This "romantic love" is given its due when Orlando and Rosalind fall in love at first sight. It might be noted that only a few words are exchanged between them before the shaft of Eros finds its mark. This view of love is later enhanced when Shakespeare has Phebe quote Marlowe, "Who ever lov'd that lov'd not at first sight?" (Act III, Scene 5). Later, this view of romantic love will be satirized when Oliver falls in love with Celia, literally at first sight (Act IV, Scene 3).

Still to come are Shakespeare's considerations of idealized and pastoral love. When all the characters finally come together in the fantasy Forest of Arden, the many different types of love are fully explored and exploited for serious and for comic effects. Shakespeare will also focus later on the sexual love that Touchstone feels for Audrey, and, here, this scene introduces Touchstone, who is an "original" with Shakespeare. As a touchstone was used in Elizabethan times to determine the purity of silver and gold, so Shakespeare uses this character to determine the sincerity of the beliefs of each character in the play. One can make a good case of the thesis that it is *Touchstone*, and not Jaques, who is the best critic of the characters within this play.

Le Beau, judging by his elevated speech and dress, is a dandy. As such, he is satirized by Shakespeare not only for his speech and dress, but also for his mannerisms in this scene.

Finally, this scene foreshadows Orlando's subsequent departure from the ducal estates to the Forest of Arden. For Orlando, as well as for many of the key characters in this scene, nothing seems to work out for him — or for them. An uneasiness pervades the tranquil setting. What is natural seems *un*natural, and in the Forest of Arden, in contrast, what might seem unnatural seems very natural. In the real world, the characters must try and control themselves in a world that tries to control them. Only in the wild, fantastic, pastoral setting of the Forest of Arden can the characters give full vent to their feelings.

ACT I – SCENE 3

Summary

Shortly afterward in the palace, we hear Rosalind confess her love for Orlando to Celia; she begs that Celia love him also for her sake. The girls' talk of love, however, is interrupted by the duke's furious entrance. "Full of anger," he tells Rosalind that she is to be banished from the palace within ten days: "If that thou be'st found/So near our public court as twenty miles,/ Thou diest for it."

Rosalind protests that she is no traitor to him, and Celia begs her father to relent, but he is adamant. He repeats his threat once more, then leaves them. Celia is determined that the two girls will not be separated, and she proposes to go with Rosalind to join Rosalind's deposed father in the Forest of Arden. But when they both realize that they are fearful of the dangers of the journey, they decide to disguise themselves: Rosalind will dress as a boy, taking the name of "Ganymede," and Celia will dress as a young farm girl and use "Aliena" as her name. Moreover, Celia will convince Touchstone, one of her father's jesters, to join them. Happy and excited, she and Rosalind go off to pack their "jewels and wealth" to take with them on their flight.

Commentary

Here, Duke Frederick's villainy is fully revealed. He banished Rosalind from his court because she reminds the people of her exiled father: "Thou art thy father's daughter. There's enough!" He suffers no remorse when his daughter, Celia, states her intent of accompanying Rosalind. He tells Celia, "You are a fool."

Thus, the stage is set for Rosalind to join her father in the Forest of Arden. There can be little doubt that Orlando will soon join the group, for we have seen that Oliver's temper is much like Frederick's.

The plot is further complicated at this point with a dramatic device that was a favorite of Elizabethan audiences; when the two girls decide to go forth alone in the world, they go in *disguise*. Rosalind chooses to go as "Ganymede" (the name of a Trojan youth abducted to Olympus, where he was made the cupbearer of the gods and became immortal), and Celia chooses to go as "Aliena." Shakespeare takes both names from the novel *Rosalynde* (1590) by Thomas Lodge.

That the girls should take Touchstone with them serves two key purposes. First, the ploy is used so that a masterful critic of society will be in the Forest of Arden, and there he will, ironically and unexpectedly, fall in love with Audrey, an earthy, country woman; second, the fact that Touchstone will accompany the girls makes him a favorite of the audience; he is a brave and loyal friend to the two heroines, damsels in distress.

Celia's concluding lines — "Now go we in content/ To liberty and not to banishment" — foreshadow the mood expressed in the following scene by Duke Senior, Rosalind's father. This mood of freedom, the prevailing mood of the Forest of Arden, will be expressed throughout the play.

ACT II – SCENE 1

Summary

In the Forest of Arden, Duke Senior expresses satisfaction with the pastoral life. He tells them that he:

> Finds tongues in trees, books in the running brooks,
> Sermons in stones, and good in every thing.
>
> (16-17)

As they prepare for the hunt, he confesses that he is troubled that they must kill the deer "in their own confines," but his mood changes when he hears the First Lord's account of the lamentations of the melancholy Jaques, who lies near a brook, reflecting philosophically on the sad fate of a wounded deer. Amused by Jaques's excessive sentimentality, the duke asks to be brought to the spot, for he enjoys arguing playfully with Jaques.

Commentary

In this scene, Duke Senior enlarges on an idea expressed by Celia at the end of Act I. He raises the question of the pastoral life being superior to that of the city. This thought colors the mood of the scenes set in the Forest of Arden and for the remainder of the play: "Are not these woods/ More free from peril than the envious court?" This sentiment will be echoed time and again in various ways.

The duke's speech is a satire on a commonplace view held at that time by many city dwellers. "Sweet are the uses of adversity," the duke says; this is an exaggerated view of the pastoral life, where he must live in exile, but later in this scene, Jaques, a critic of the world at large, extends this already exaggerated view and contends sarcastically that the pastoral life also endorses the notion that it is necessary:

> To frighten the animals and to kill them up
> In their assign'd and native dwelling place.
>
> (62-63)

It is evident that Jaques's view of the pastoral life is not at all practical. However, the view is typical of Jaques in that it is a shallow generalization of the situation in which he finds himself.

It is also important to note that Duke Senior, while enjoying Jaques's company, is not overly impressed with Jaques's philosophy: "I love to cope [muse playfully with] him in these sullen fits,/ For then he's full of matter." This is the first clue that Jaques is not to be taken too seriously. Jaques always thinks that his thoughts are profound, but they are rather ordinary and are always generalized.

Shakespeare is satirizing both views here: Duke Senior's – that everything in nature is good – and Jaques's – that nature is good only when man is not around to evoke change. Both views were popular at the time.

ACT II – SCENE 2

Summary

In this scene, Frederick discovers that Celia and Rosalind are gone and that Touchstone is also missing. A lord tells him that the cousins were overheard praising Orlando; he suggests that they may be in his company. Frederick then commands that Orlando or – in the event of Orlando's absence – that Oliver be brought to him.

Commentary

This scene serves two purposes. First, it offers a way for Oliver to be sent to the Forest of Arden, where he will meet with the other exiled characters. Now, only Orlando and Adam remain behind, yet very shortly, both of them will leave for the Forest of Arden. We realize, therefore, that soon all of the main characters will arrive there, and the main action of the play will begin. Second, this scene stands in juxtaposition to the preceding scene. Whereas the preceding scene was one of pensive tranquility, Scene 2 is harsh; it is filled with tension and vengefulness.

The counterbalancing of scenes, one contrasting with the other, is a dramatic device much used by Shakespeare. In this particular play, the grouping of scenes without a hint of serious movement has led some critics to compare these elements to those found in the masque, an elaborate, lighthearted and extravagantly costumed entertainment which was much in vogue in the sixteenth century.

ACT II – SCENE 3

Summary

Arriving home, Orlando meets Adam, who tells him that news of his triumph in the wrestling match has spread and that Oliver is plotting to burn down Orlando's sleeping quarters that very night. Failing that, Adam says, Oliver will try to murder Orlando by some other means. He warns Orlando to leave immediately. When Orlando protests that he has no way to make a living, the old servant presses upon him his life's savings of five hundred crowns and begs him to leave, and he also begs Orlando to take him along in the young man's service. Orlando praises Adam for his devotion, then they both hurry off.

Commentary

As villains in a comedy, Oliver and Duke Frederick rank only a degree below Shakespeare's best. They never reach the level of an Iago, however, simply because they are never quite successful. Their villainy is only in thought, never in deed. Duke Frederick may have usurped his brother's lands, but he cannot get rid of his brother's influence, as evidenced in Rosalind's relationship with Celia and vice versa, when Rosalind is forced to flee from the ducal court.

It is interesting to note that old Adam, pictured here as goodness personified, serves as a counter-balance to the villainy of Oliver and Frederick. Falling in the middle of these extremes are the more realistic characters of Orlando, Rosalind, and Celia.

Orlando's discussion of the "antique world" and his looking forward to a better day echoes the tranquil mood of the Forest of Arden, established by Duke Senior in Act II, Scene 1.

At this point in the play, all of the major characters who are representative of courtly life are either in the Forest of Arden or on their way there. It is now time to meet their counterparts from the country.

ACT II – SCENE 4

Summary

After we left Orlando and Adam hurrying toward the Forest of Arden in the last scene, we now meet a trio of weary travelers – Rosalind, dressed as a young man, and Celia, and Touchstone; they have finally reached the forest. As they pause to rest, a young shepherd, Silvius, enters, solemnly describing his unrequited love for Phebe to his friend Corin. So distraught by love is Silvius that he suddenly breaks off his conversation and runs away, crying "O Phebe, Phebe, Phebe!" Touchstone now hails Corin in a preposterously superior manner, but Rosalind intervenes and courteously requests food and shelter. Corin explains that he is *not* his own master: he merely serves another. His landlord, he explains, plans to sell his cottage, his flocks, and his pasturage to Silvius, who is so preoccupied with Phebe that he "little cares for buying any thing." Rosalind quickly commissions Corin to make the purchase on behalf of Celia and herself, and they ask Corin to stay on, at a better wage, as their own shepherd.

Commentary

The opening exposition in this scene establishes the setting for the audience. Touchstone's remark, "When I was at home, I was in a better place . . ." focuses immediately on the theme of town life versus country life. It also reflects Touchstone's realistic outlook, a viewpoint of his which is used throughout the play as a contrast to the romantic notions of the other characters. For example, note his speech in this scene where he remembers a romance of his own (lines 46-56). Most likely, it never happened at all, but it is humorously amusing. His kissing a club, his thinking of a cow's teats when he took his beloved's hands, and his wooing a "peacod" – all of these are too preposterous for us to fully believe, yet his boastful speech is a perfect contrast to the pastoral notions of Silvius, while at the same time it is a clever parody on the romantic notions of Rosalind. Additionally, in giving two cods (peapods) to his mistress (an Elizabethan term for sweetheart), Touchstone parodies Rosalind's giving a necklace to Orlando and, at the same time, he satirizes Silvius's concept of pastoral love. And of historical note here, it is of interest that lovers in those days would often risk tearing a peacod from the vine without accidentally tearing it open. If successful, they would give it to their beloved as a sign of faithful devotion. Touchstone, in using the peacod to represent his love, foreshadows Orlando's use of Ganymede in place of Rosalind as a representative of his love.

Finally, perhaps we should mention Rosalind's purchase of a sheepstead; this bit of business brings a bit of realism to an otherwise unrealistic play. We are surprised at the quick financial transaction. It is broad comedy, whether or not Shakespeare meant it to be, and it is always a source of laughter.

ACT II – SCENE 5

Summary

Amiens, Jaques, and several lords of Duke Senior are gathered in another part of the forest. Amiens has been singing, and Jaques urges him to continue while the others sing along. Amiens does so and orders the others to lay out a meal under the trees.

Jaques has been avoiding the duke all day, calling him "too disputable [argumentative] for my company." He contributes a cynical verse of his own composition to Amiens's song, then lies down to rest while Amiens goes to seek the duke.

Commentary

The pastoral songs in this play serve several purposes. They restate the theme of town life versus country life; town life, they envision as being dismal and corrupt, while country life is fair and clean. Shakespeare, it should be noted, satirizes both views. The songs also serve to break up the "tide-like" action of the scenes; in other words, they bring variety to a scene in the forest being followed by a scene at court, followed by one in the forest, and so forth.

Finally, the songs are part of the masque elements in this play. This genre of the masque was characterized by quickly changed scenes and tableaux with emphasis upon elaborate costumes and scenery, representative of mythological or pastoral elements. Dance and music were also essential elements. The use of the masque elements here culminates with the entrance of Hymen (the god of marriage) and the climactic triple wedding scene.

The primary purpose of this scene seems to focus on Shakespeare's delineation of the character of Jaques. Jaques is always argumentative, indiscriminately taking the opposing view, never pleased with anything or anybody. He likes to think of himself as being profound, but his thoughts are of a commonplace nature and are usually vitriolic. His humor is ironic. For example, he comments that Duke Senior is too argumentative, whereas he himself is the most argumentative character in the play.

Jaques's song serves as a rebuke to the pastoral sentiment of Amiens's song. Jaques, who insists that Amiens sing, afterwards criticizes what he himself wanted to hear. Again, it is to be expected that Jaques will take the opposing view in an argument, regardless of its merit. Throughout the play, he rails against the pastoral view of life but, finally, he is the only character who chooses to remain in the forest, while the others return to the town as soon as possible.

ACT II – SCENE 6

Summary

In the last scene, we noted that a meal was being prepared for the duke and his men; in this scene, in contrast, no meal awaits Orlando and Adam as they wander through the forest. Adam says that he is too weak from hunger to go on, but his master comforts him by promising to find him a shelter and, afterwards, some food.

Commentary

This scene serves to establish the fact that Orlando and Adam have arrived in the Forest of Arden, and it prepares us for Orlando's meeting with Duke Senior and the duke's company in the next scene.

Because Orlando attends Adam so loyally and attentively, it raises the audience's estimation of him. He is young, but he exhibits a noble character, probably inherited from his father. As always, we note his concern and courtesy toward others. He is a gentle, good youth.

ACT II – SCENE 7

Summary

Duke Senior, Rosalind's father, who is searching for Jaques, arrives on the scene and unexpectedly meets Jaques. Jaques describes, with evident delight, his meeting with Touchstone. He says that he wishes that *he* were a "fool" (and dressed in an identifiable coat of motley) so that he might be able "as the wind,/ To blow on whom I please," exercising the fool's prerogative of speaking his mind freely to expose the world's abuses. But Jaques, as the duke notes, has a libertine past; this hardly qualifies him to reproach others for their failings. Their discussion abruptly ends when Orlando enters with his sword drawn. "Forbear," he cries, "and eat no more" – although the meal has scarcely begun. (This in itself is high comedy.) Orlando is calmed by the duke's courteous welcome, and he apologizes and sheathes his sword. Then, begging the duke to put off dining until his return, he goes to fetch Adam. This episode inspires Jaques's account of the seven ages of man.

This extended philosophical statement has since become one of the most celebrated speeches in the Shakespearean canon. Most learned people in the Western world recognize the lines "All the world's a stage/ And all the men and women merely players. . . ." The point of view of the speech is colored by Jaques's cynicism, yet the speech itself has such imaginative power that it transcends Jaques's melancholy and causes one to pause and contemplate this schematic evaluation of man. According to Jaques, these are the seven ages of man:

(1) the infant: "mewling and puking in the nurse's arms. . . ."

(2) the schoolboy: "whining . . . with his satchel/ And shining morning face, creeping like a snail,/ Unwilling to school. . . ."

(3) the lover: "sighing like a furnace, with a woeful ballad . . . to his mistress' eyebrow."

(4) the soldier: "full of strange oaths . . . bearded . . ./ Jealous in honour, sudden, and quick in quarrel,/ Seeking the bubble's reputation/ Even in the cannon's mouth."

(5) the justice (or judge): "in fair round belly with good capon lin'd [an allusion to the bribing of judges with gifts of poultry] . . . eyes severe and beard of formal cut,/ Full of wise saws [sayings] and modern instances [examples]. . . ."

(6) the dotard (or absent-minded old man): "lean and slipper'd . . ./ With spectacles on nose and [money] pouch on side,/ His youthful hose, well saved, a world too wide/ For his shrunk shank; and his big manly voice,/ Turning again toward childish treble, pipes/ And whistles in his sound.

(7) the senile, sick elder: "[reduced to] second childishness and mere oblivion,/ Sans [without] teeth, sans eyes, sans taste, sans everything."

Despite Jaques's surface cynicism, Shakespeare's poetry is impressively sensitive and beautiful. This is Shakespeare at his most brilliant best.

Orlando returns, just as Jacques finishes; he is carrying Adam, and as they begin eating, Amiens sings "Blow, blow, thou winter wind." When the song ends, Duke Senior warmly welcomes "the good Sir Roland's son" (Orlando has whispered his identity to his host) and welcomes Adam as well. The scene ends happily; the duke takes old Adam's hand, and the group sets off for the duke's cave.

Commentary

In no scene is the exaggerated melancholy and simple cynicism of Jaques more clearly evident than here. He opens his meeting with Rosalind's father by relating an encounter he has just had with

Touchstone. In the encounter, Jaques was completely taken in by the clown. He was totally unaware that Touchstone was parodying Jaques's own style of speech. Instead, Jaques found Touchstone's remarks to be so profound that he wishes that he could be a fool himself. Touchstone's comments, thus, foreshadow Jaques's well-known "Seven Ages of Man" speech:

> 'Tis but an hour ago since it was nine;
> And after one hour more 'twill be eleven;
> And so, from hour to hour, we ripe and ripe
> And then, from hour to hour, we rot and rot;
> And thereby hangs a tale.
>
> (24-28)

One might also note that the sun dial which Touchstone produces is an unlikely, absurd instrument to use in a forest. That Jaques would use the sun dial to time his laughter, exactly the duration of one hour, underscores his ridiculous behavior, as if he or anyone could laugh for a specific amount of time.

Jaques's character, unfortunately, has often been misunderstood. The duke, for example, calls him a "libertine." The word at that time did not carry the moral connotations it does today. Then, it merely meant a man of the world. It must also be remembered that the duke likes to argue with Jaques (II.i.68-69), and in this scene, he is drawing Jaques out to discover what Jaques is thinking. He challenges Jaques's claim to be a reformer of society. Jaques accepts the challenge. The duke, of course, is being whimsically humorous and asks Jaques what he would ". . . disgorge into the general world," but Jaques obviously misses the duke's humorously exaggerated attack on his overblown pomposity. Instead, he immediately seizes the bait and rants on about how he would save society. In doing so, Jaques not only has the last word, but he also absurdly satirizes late sixteenth-century satirists.

To some critics, the remark made by Orlando, "yet am I inland bred/ And know some nature," seems to contradict his speech in Act I, Scene 1. This is not the case. Both words "civility" and "nurture" meant good breeding in the general use of the term, rather than in the modern use of politeness, and it was considered good breeding to salute those whom one met. Orlando obviously does not salute when he makes his entrance. The duke challenges this impropriety.

Jaques's division of life into seven ages was a proverbial, as well as a popular, idea in Elizabethan England. It is an ancient idea, and Shakespeare makes reference to it in *The Merchant of Venice* (Act I, Scene 1) and in *Macbeth* (Act V, Scene 5). Moreover, the speech is consistent with Jaques's character; it is highly generalized (the kind of pigeon-hole categorizing that his mind would be fascinated with), and it is expressed in an untutored, insightful manner. Without Jaques realizing it, he becomes a one-man Chorus, delivering a keen philosophical discourse in capsule form. As a counter-balance to this philosophizing, both Jaques and Touchstone keep the audience from becoming too contemplative and also from becoming too involved with the fantasy of the forest; they serve as reminders that Duke Senior, Rosalind, and Orlando are playing only temporary parts in a masquerade in an unusual setting.

ACT III – SCENE 1

Summary

At court, Duke Frederick threatens Oliver that if he does not bring back Orlando "dead or living/ Within this twelvemonth . . . turn thou no more/ To seek a living in our territory." In that event, Oliver's possessions will revert to Frederick. "I never loved my brother in my life," Oliver swears. "More villain thou," Frederick snaps back and orders his men to make sure that Oliver leaves the palace.

Commentary

This scene completes the action initiated in Act II, Scene 2 – that is, Oliver must go to the Forest of Arden, where he will eventually meet with the other characters, and it is ironic that Frederick calls Oliver a villain for not loving his brother; Frederick is blatantly guilty of the same want of feeling for *his* brother.

ACT III – SCENE 2

Summary

Orlando has problems that are quite different from his brother's. Oliver must find Orlando; Orlando would like to seek Rosalind if he could, but since he cannot, he has been spending his days hanging love poems on trees and carving the name "Rosalind" onto trees. As a result, when this scene opens, Orlando is about to decorate more trees in this manner when Corin and Touchstone enter. They begin to discuss the relative merits of the life in the country and at court, but are interrupted by Rosalind (still disguised as Ganymede), who comes in reading one of the poems. "From the east to western Ind," she reads, "No jewel is like Rosalind." Touchstone is not impressed, and so he parodies the "false gallop" of the verse with a poem of his own.

Celia joins them, reading yet another love poem and orders Touchstone and Corin to leave them to themselves. Celia intimates to Rosalind that she knows who the writer of the poems is, and Rosalind begs to be told. Upon hearing that it is Orlando who has probably written the poems, she asks so many questions that Celia cannot find time to answer them all, but Celia does tell Rosalind that she saw the poet in a forester's garb, lying "under a tree, like a dropped acorn." At that moment, Orlando and Jaques enter. They spend a few minutes verbally sparring (calling one another "Signior Love" and "Monsieur Melancholy"), and then Jaques takes his leave.

The lovers now confront one another, but Orlando does not, of course, realize that he is speaking to Rosalind in disguise, and so she resolves to "speak to him like a saucy lackey and under that habit play the knave with him." Thus she gaily banters with him about such subjects as time, women, and a certain lovesick youth who haunts the forest carving the name "Rosalind" on tree trunks. Orlando freely confesses that it is *he* who is that lovesick fellow and, "Ganymede" generously offers to "cure" Orlando of his love-sickness: Orlando must pretend that young Ganymede is the fair Rosalind and Orlando must visit Ganymede's cottage daily to court Ganymede, who will impersonate Rosalind. Like a goodhearted comrade, Ganymede promises his friend Orlando that he will cure him of his lunacy. He will show Orlando just how silly women are; Orlando consents. "With all my heart, good youth," he tells Ganymede, he will attempt the cure while Ganymede will, like a coquette "like him, now loathe him; then entertain him, then forswear him; now weep for him, then spit at him." But Ganymede insists that Orlando must steel himself for the cure; he tells Orlando that he must not call him "good youth." "Nay . . . call me Rosalind," Ganymede orders. Once more, the lovesick Orlando agrees.

Commentary

Orlando's hanging his verses in the trees reflects a commonplace convention in the pastoral genre of Elizabethan writers. Another convention of the time was to carve verses or names into the bark of trees. Here, Shakespeare is satirizing these conventions.

Later, in the encounter between Corin and Touchstone, it is interesting to note that Corin uses the respectful and formal words "master" and "you" in addressing the clown, while Touchstone condescendingly says "shepherd" and uses the familiar pronoun "thou." Each is amused by the other's quick mind – Touchstone is admired because of his wit, and Corin is admired because of his rustic answers. Neither takes the other too seriously, however.

The role of Corin, one might note, is included as a foil to Silvius. Corin is a real shepherd who knows something about sheep – that is, about shearing and herding; in addition, he has some difficulty expressing himself, much like William and Audrey, who also are representatives of true country life. Yet his thoughts, while very often seeming "homely," are shrewd. In contrast, Silvius (and later Phebe, also) is a representative from the pastoral genre of literature. He is dressed like a shepherd, and he wanders about all the day talking of love, but he knows *nothing* of tending sheep. Shakespeare uses this contrast, obviously, to point out the difference between the two shepherds and, more important, to satirize the precious, romantic idealism of the pastoral genre.

Also associated with this, there is a set of contrasts in Touchstone's poem and Orlando's poetry. Touchstone's poem is in a realistic vein, and it satirizes the romantic notions of Orlando's poetry. At that time, a great many love poems were composed, and many of them were as amateurishly bad as Orlando's. Many, of course, were worse.

The pact between Rosalind (Ganymede) and Orlando leads to some of the most humorous moments in the play. This dramatic gimmick was not original with Shakespeare (it was borrowed from Thomas Lodge's novel *Rosalynde*), but Shakespeare embellished it and complicated it with disguises and, from the first production, it was a sure-fire success with Elizabethan audiences, who always enjoyed intricate plots and intrigue. Here, the heroine finds herself in a position to hear her lover extol her virtues and his love for her without his being aware of her identity. The dramatic irony is a touch of brilliance.

ACT III – SCENE 3

Summary

There are other, less romantic lovers in the Forest of Arden. For example, there is the "poetic" and philosophical Touchstone and the earthy Audrey. Yielding to instinct, Touchstone has wooed and has finally won Audrey, perhaps Shakespeare's most dull-witted country wench. The pair hurry along to meet Sir Oliver Martext, the vicar of the neighboring village, and are followed by Jaques, who is, as might be expected, amused by the incongruous pair. When Sir Oliver arrives, they discover that there is no one to give the bride away, so Jaques offers his services, but he recommends that they be married by a priest as "this fellow will but join you together as they join wainscot." Touchstone, however, would prefer it that way because, as he says in an aside, "not being well married, it will be a good excuse for me hereafter to leave my wife." So he decides to find a proper person to marry him and Audrey, and he goes off with Audrey and Jaques, merrily singing and leaving behind a bemused Sir Oliver.

Commentary

Audrey, very much like Corin and, later, like William, is a realistic, country person. All are contrasts to the pastoral lovers,

Silvius and Phebe. The relationship between Audrey and Touch-stone is very realistic; this couple is concerned with sexual love, not with chaste, romantic, "poetic" love. Touchstone says, "We must be married, or we must live in bawdry." Contrast this realism with the verbal excesses of Silvius: "Then shall you know the wounds invisible/ That love's keen arrows make," Silvius says to Phebe. His words are colored with an abundance of poetic "romance"; occasionally, Orlando also reaches these poetic heights.

Touchstone's wooing of Audrey is particularly humorous because she *never* understands the sparring verbal wit of Touchstone at all. This doesn't bother her unduly, however, and it is her very lack of concern which amuses Jaques, who also finds Touchstone's utterances full of profound wisdom, still one more rich vein of humor in this merry comedy.

ACT III – SCENE 4

Summary

When this scene opens, Rosalind is at the point of tears; she is sitting in the forest with Celia, waiting for Orlando, who has not kept his first appointment for the "love cure." Celia teases her friend about Orlando's unreliability, but then she points out that Orlando is probably helping take care of matters for Rosalind's father, Duke Senior. Rosalind reveals that she has met her father in the forest, but she says that he did not recognize her in her disguise. Her father's plight and his presence in the forest doesn't concern her unduly, however; she can think only of Orlando. Happily, Corin comes along, offering them, and us, some diversion: a "pageant" of love – Silvius courting the scornful Phebe.

Commentary

This scene clearly shows us the depth of Rosalind's love for Orlando. That Celia is not in love at this time and is practical in her advice tends to make Rosalind's love seem all the more intense, of course. There is a certain degree of melodramatic pathos to the situation, and for that reason we are ready to laugh at the overindulgent

CROWN BOOKS #910

```
CROWN BOOKS #910
---
11829    52         F      18:50     03/24/98
REFUNDS WITHIN 30 DAYS WITH RECEIPT ONLY
           MAGAZINE SALES FINAL
           PUBLISHER
CROWN      CROWN         CROWN
PRICE
PRICE      SAVINGS       SAVINGS
CLIFF AS YOU LIKE IT
1@    3.75  0822000075   10%         3.38
SUBTOTAL            $    3.38
SALES TAX @ 7.75%   $    0.26
TOTAL               $    3.64
TENDERED Cash       $    4.00
CHANGE              $    0.36

YOUR SAVINGS AT CROWN... $ 0.37
```

"love" of Silvius for Phebe. Corin's invitation to the girls to watch the couple is a clever bit of dramatic balancing; his realistic speech offers a refreshing contrast to the romantic verbosity of the girls.

ACT III – SCENE 5

Summary

As Rosalind, Celia, and Corin secretly watch Silvius pleading for Phebe's favor, we hear her warn him to "come not thou near me." She treats Silvius with utter disdain, but Silvius insists that she will understand his torment when she too is in love. She is not to be persuaded, however, and Rosalind suddenly interrupts the pair and severely chides Phebe for her unresponsiveness to Silvius's pleadings; she recommends, rather unflatteringly, that Phebe take what is offered. "Sell when you can; you are not for all markets." That is her advice to the disdainful shepherdess.

Phebe suddenly becomes unaccountably captivated by the superbly disguised Rosalind; the young "man" before her is commanding and disarmingly magnetic. Rosalind and the others leave, and Phebe is left alone with Silvius; she muses about the location of the manly Ganymede's cottage. He *is* attractive, she thinks, and thus her feelings vacillate between being utterly undone by this "pretty youth" and between being angry at him, the "peevish boy," for his sharp tongue. Since Ganymede is gone, however, she consents to accept the company of Silvius because he *can* "talk of love so well." Then off they go to write a taunting letter to Ganymede to repay him for his impertinence.

Commentary

The encounter between Silvius and Phebe is a satire on conventional love – that is, the lady feels that she is superior to her lover, and her lover, in anguish, swears to die if he is denied her love. The scene also satirizes Silvius and Phebe as representatives of the pastoral genre.

The plot, which is already complicated by disguises, is even further complicated in this scene when Phebe falls in love with an attractive "personage" who she thinks is a young man, when "he" is really Rosalind, who in reality was being played on Shakespeare's stage by a young man. Elizabethan audiences, however, loved this kind of whimsical gender gymnastics, and even today, this kind of drag masquerade is sure-fire comedy, provided of course that it is done in broad humor.

ACT IV – SCENE 1

Summary

While Celia listens to their arguing, Rosalind (still disguised as Ganymede) and Jaques banter about his melancholy; Jaques maintains that it is "good to be sad and say nothing," while Rosalind maintains that if one is sad *and* silent, one might as well "be a post." When Orlando finally arrives (late for his appointment), Jaques bids Ganymede goodbye. Turning to Orlando, Ganymede berates him for his tardiness, then lovingly invites him to woo Ganymede *as if* he were Orlando's beloved Rosalind; in turn, Ganymede will tease and taunt Orlando as if he were Rosalind. Ganymede wittily instructs Orlando thus in the wily ways of love and women. "You shall never take her without her answer, unless you take her without her tongue," Orlando is warned. At this point, Orlando says that he must leave to attend Duke Senior at dinner, but he promises to return at two o'clock. After he has gone, Celia accuses Rosalind of speaking ill of women; she suggests that perhaps Rosalind should have her doublet and hose "plucked over [her] head in order to show the world what the bird hath done to her own nest." Rosalind, in answer, says that love has made her a bit mad; she has such a love for Orlando that she cannot bear to be out of his sight. With that, she leaves and goes to "find a shadow and sigh till he come." Celia decides to take a nap.

Commentary

It is easy fun for the witty and clever Rosalind to tease Jaques, and while she does so, we should be aware that she also satirizes many Elizabethan Englishmen who traveled to the Continent acquiring affected behavior. Jaques of course, is unaware of her satirical teasing, and so he continues on in his sober manner.

Other clues as to Jaques's character are provided in this scene when Rosalind describes him as speaking with a "lisp"; to speak with a lisp meant that he spoke with an affected mannerism, probably acquired on his travels to the Continent. She also chides Jaques for turning his back, as it were, on his native country and wearing "strange suits."

Orlando's entrance here has been much discussed. Obviously, Jaques and Rosalind are downstage (near the audience) and begin moving upstage, probably when Jaques decides to leave Rosalind since she insists on talking "in blank verse," meaning in the poetic language of love. Jaques notices Orlando's entrance and acknowledges his greeting. Rosalind pretends *not* to notice his entrance and moves along, continuing to talk to Jaques. As they move upstage, then, Orlando moves downstage. Thus when Jaques exits, Rosalind turns and pretends surprise.

In the encounter between Ganymede and Orlando, Rosalind almost gives herself away because she is so delighted that she is being wooed by Orlando, who, of course, is unaware of her identity. It is Rosalind's utter delight that gives the scene an extraordinary depth of sweetness and gentle humor.

In the mock wedding scene, it is important to note that Rosalind's fondest wish is almost made a reality; she is putting the vows of marriage upon Orlando's lips, and she herself replies, "I do take thee, Orlando, for my husband." Even in a comedy such as this, such vows are serious. Rosalind realizes this just in time and teases Orlando that men are "like April when they woo" and that they are "December when they are wed." If she was, as Celia accused her of being earlier, harsh on women, she now turns her witty jesting toward the men. Furthermore, she warns the lovesick Orlando that she, the "Rosalind" of his dreams, will be "more jealous of [him] than a Barbary cock-pigeon over his hen, more clamorous than a parrot against rain, more new-fangled than an ape, more giddy in my desires than a monkey." All this is possible. She is every bit as in love with Orlando as he is with her. Lovers, she is saying, are a bit mad; she realizes this truth about herself and, thus, she half-teasingly, half-seriously, promises him that Rosalind will "weep for nothing, like Diana in the fountain" and that Rosalind will weep

38

when Orlando is "dispos'd to be merry." Rosalind-as-wife will be no
soft, pliant, submissive lady. Rosalind will, in fact, be herself – high-
spirited and bewitchingly exciting.

ACT IV – SCENE 2

Summary

Several of Duke Senior's followers have been hunting, and one
of them has killed a deer. Jaques suggests that they "present him to
the Duke, like a Roman conqueror," and they carry out their slaugh-
tered trophy, singing "What shall he have that kill'd the deer?"

Commentary

This scene is a sequel to the last scene. Jaques again assumes
his pose as critic-at-large. It is characteristic of him to criticize a
song before it is sung, and this song, one might note, is concerned
with the horns of the deer. This is a sexual reference to a man's being a cuckold – that is, the husband of an unfaithful wife, a situation
which the Elizabethan audiences never tired of as a source for comedy. Throughout all of literature, the cuckolded husband has been
the butt of many comedies.

ACT IV – SCENE 3

Summary

It is past two o'clock, and Orlando has not arrived for his meeting with Ganymede. Silvius does arrive, however, bringing Phebe's
letter to Ganymede, and Rosalind playfully pretends that it is, as
the illiterate shepherd supposed, full of invective, and she teasingly
accuses Silvius of writing it because it is a "man's invention and his
hand." But when she stops and actually reads the letter aloud, even
the gullible Silvius realizes that the note is, in actuality, a *love*
poem – to Ganymede. Silvius is ordered to return to Phebe with this
message: "if she loves me [Ganymede], I charge her to love thee; if
she will not, I will never have her unless thou entreat for her."

A stranger arrives onstage next. It is Oliver; he has come in search of Ganymede, and he presents "him" with a token from Orlando, a bloody handkerchief. He explains that Orlando, while walking in the forest, discovered Oliver sleeping under an oak. A snake had coiled itself around Oliver's neck, but because it was frightened by Orlando's entrance, it slid away. Nearby, a hungry lioness waited for Oliver to awaken before pouncing upon him. After debating with himself whether to save Oliver or leave him to certain death, Orlando fought and killed the lioness. Oliver, awakening to see his brother risking his life to save him, realized that his brother loved him deeply, and so his hatred for Orlando changed to love. Now reconciled, the brothers proceeded to Duke Senior's encampment, where Oliver discovered that the lioness had torn Orlando's flesh. He has brought the handkerchief which Orlando used to bind his wounded arm, and he presents it to Ganymede with apologies for Orlando's broken promise — that is, he presents it "unto the shepherd youth/ That he [Orlando] in sport doth call his Rosalind." At this point, Ganymede swoons. As he is helped up and led away, he insists — although not very convincingly — that his fainting was merely an act, an unconscious reaction by his persona, "Rosalind."

Commentary

In the brief exchange between Ganymede and Silvius, at first Rosalind isn't sure if Silvius is aware of the contents of the letter. She only *pretends* to read it, therefore, and gives a false interpretation of the contents. Finally, she asks Silvius if the letter was written by him. It is a clever ruse to discover whether or not he is aware of the contents. Realizing that Silvius is ignorant of the message, Rosalind, with compassion, reads the letter aloud (for the benefit of the audience) and attempts to misconstrue its meaning. But Silvius is not so easily duped; Rosalind, therefore, drops all pretense and reads the full letter.

It is interesting here to note that Celia expresses pity for Silvius, but Rosalind, in keeping with her manly characterization of Ganymede, sneers at pity. Likewise, Ganymede's command to Phebe, via Silvius, is in keeping with the indifference shown to Phebe in Act III, Scene 5.

When Oliver makes his entrance, he says, "Good morrow, fair ones." The use of the word "fair" was in keeping with the times when men could also be described as being "fair." Certainly Oliver is unaware of Rosalind's disguise, as evidenced by his use of "you" in line 85, where he describes Rosalind as being both "fair" and "a boy" and where he describes Celia as being "a woman" and "browner than her brother."

Oliver's sudden conversion from hate to love for his brother, one should note, though it might strain the credulity of a modern audience, was a commonplace device in Elizabethan plays. Sudden conversions can also be found in, for example, Shakespeare's *Measure for Measure*, *All's Well That Ends Well*, and *Cymbeline*.

When Oliver tells Ganymede about Orlando's wound, Ganymede faints, but Celia, being quick-witted, remembers to call her cousin "Ganymede." However, Celia does slip when she inadvertently refers to Ganymede as "Cousin Ganymede" in line 160. Luckily, Oliver misses this error on Celia's part. Rosalind, on awakening, resumes the game that she is playing with Oliver, and the comic masquerade continues as she tells him to tell Orlando that Ganymede "counterfeited" so well that when he heard that Orlando had been wounded, he *swooned*, as if he were, really, the fair, faint-hearted Rosalind.

ACT V – SCENE 1

Summary

When the scene opens, Audrey is fretting about her postponed marriage; "Faith, the priest [Oliver Martext] was good enough," she whines, but Touchstone changes the subject by mentioning a youth "here in the forest" who has claimed Audrey as his own. This rustic character, William, now appears, and in answer to Touchstone's question "Art thou wise?" he replies, "Ay, Sir, I have a pretty wit." To this, Touchstone responds by quoting a saying beginning "The fool doth think he is wise." Thus, Touchstone quickly reduces William to a state of stupefaction. William meekly goes away, and Corin arrives with word that Touchstone is wanted by Aliena and Ganymede.

Commentary

Note that in this scene, Touchstone, in addressing William, uses the condescending pronoun "thou," while William uses the more respectful pronoun "you." Here, William, like Audrey and Corin, is used by Shakespeare to contrast the real country characters with the pastoral lovers, Silvius and Phebe. Characteristic of real country people, we see, is an inability to easily express themselves. The longest sentence used by William, for example, contains six words, and most of his sentences are three to four words in length. As an additional dramatic point, one should realize that in this encounter, William takes the remarks of Touchstone quite seriously, even though he doesn't fully comprehend them. In addition, Audrey also has trouble following Touchstone's wit, for she is just as simple as William is. However, at the beginning of the scene, Audrey *does* realize that it will be no easy matter to get Touchstone before the altar.

ACT V – SCENE 2

Summary

Oliver has fallen in love with Aliena at first glance, and he tells Orlando that she has consented to marry him. He vows to give to Orlando his "father's house and all the revenue that was old Sir Roland's . . . and here live and die a shepherd." Orlando approves of the marriage, and it is then scheduled for the following day. Rosalind, as Ganymede, enters and tells of the whirlwind courtship of Aliena and Oliver in which they "no sooner looked but they loved." When Orlando confesses his own "heart-heaviness" because he is without his own true love, Ganymede tells him that *he*, Ganymede, is knowledgeable in the art of magic and says, "If you do love Rosalind so near the heart as your gesture cries it out, when your brother marries Aliena, [then] shall you marry her [Rosalind]," and Ganymede promises to "set her before [Orlando's] eyes to-morrow, human as she is, and without any danger."

Phebe and Silvius join them then, and Phebe expresses her love for Ganymede, Silvius expresses his love for Phebe, Ganymede says that he loves "no woman," and Orlando sighs for the absent Rosalind. Ganymede promises them, however, that they shall all be married on the morrow and bids them meet her then.

Commentary

By having Orlando raise the question of Oliver's sudden love for Aliena, it is possible that Shakespeare might have been trying to apologize for his departure from Lodge's novel *Rosalynde*. In the novel, Aliena is rescued from a band of ruffians by an older brother. However, to further complicate the play with these added characters and incidents would have slowed its movement. Shakespeare was correct in omitting this plot development. Moreover, he had laid the groundwork for Oliver's sudden falling in love when Phebe earlier quoted from Marlowe on the subject of "love at first sight" (III.v.82) and when Oliver was suddenly "converted" to goodness.

This particular parody on romantic love illustrates the extremes between Silvius and Phebe on the one hand and between Oliver and Celia on the other. In contrast, true romantic love is represented in the lead characters of Orlando and Rosalind, who at least briefly engage in conversation before succumbing to romantic love.

Of interest also in this particular scene is the matter of Rosalind's claiming to be a magician, capable of divining the future. Rosalind here introduces a popular topic—magic—a subject that fascinated Elizabethan audiences. In addition, Rosalind's prophesying the multiple marriages for the next day foreshadows the arrival of Hymen in the final scene.

ACT V – SCENE 3

Summary

"To-morrow is the joyful day, Audrey," Touchstone tells his true love; "to-morrow will we be married." They are entertained then by two of the duke's pages, who sing, appropriately, "It was a lover and his lass." Afterward, Touchstone bids the minstrels "God be wi' you; and God mend your voices!"

Commentary

This dialogue between Touchstone and Audrey is a sequel to their dialogue in Act V, Scene 1. In that scene, Audrey in her simple way realized that marrying Touchstone would be no simple matter. In this scene, her "desire to be a woman of the world" seems about to be realized.

This scene is also used to give the players time to prepare for the elaborate masque in the next scene. The entrance of the two pages and their subsequent song prelude the arrival of Hymen. In the song, love is praised, especially the beauty of young love and the fact that life is short and love is for the young. It is noteworthy in this connection that unlike Jaques, Touchstone does not criticize the song *until* it is sung, and, even then, the thrust of his criticism is with the fact that "there was no great matter in the ditty," but he also adds that it was very "untunable." Until now, Jaques has never been so cleverly witty.

ACT V – SCENE 4

Summary

The climactic wedding day is now at hand. Among those present are Duke Senior, Jaques, and the three couples: Orlando and Rosalind (still disguised as Ganymede), Oliver and Celia (still masquerading as Aliena), and Phebe and Silvius. Rosalind extracts a promise from Phebe that if Phebe refuses to marry Ganymede, then Phebe will marry Silvius. Rosalind announces to the expectant company that she is prepared to unravel the entanglements. "From hence I go," she declares as she leaves with Celia, "to make these doubts all even." While they are gone, Touchstone arrives with Audrey and proceeds to entertain the company with his account of "a lie seven times removed" – the so-called Lie Direct. Here, because there was no Lie Direct, he and his opponent avoided a duel. Rosalind and Celia reappear suddenly, as if by magic, dressed as themselves. Strains of soft music usher them in, and they are led by a young man costumed as Hymen, god of marriage. The recognitions and reconciliations are quickly accomplished, and as Hymen sings a "wedlock-hymn," the couples join hands. Duke Senior welcomes a daughter and a niece, and Phebe gives her love to Silvius.

But there is yet another happy surprise in store. Jaques de Boys, the second son of Roland de Boys, enters with remarkable news: Duke Frederick, he announces, called together an army and

planned to capture and execute his brother, but at the outskirts of
the forest, he met an old, religious hermit and was converted.

> Both from his enterprise and from the world;
> His crown bequeathing to his banish'd brother,
> And all their lands restored to them again
> That were with him exil'd.
>
> (168-71)

Duke Senior welcomes the young man and invites everyone to
join in the "rustic revelry." Only Jaques begs off; instead, he will
join Frederick and his party of religious converts. With appropriate
farewells to each – Duke Senior, Orlando, Oliver, Silvius, and Touchstone – Jaques goes off, leaving the others to perform the dance that
concludes the play.

Commentary

The stage is set and the couples are assembled. Silvius and
Phebe in the characteristic pastoral style offer to die if their love is
unrequited, and Jaques, in one of his usual critical quips, comments
that Touchstone and Audrey are fools. Touchstone, of course, would
not agree; from his opening speech, he seems almost unapproach-
able. In fact, his actions are so affected in this scene, suggestive of
dramatic royalty on stage, that Touchstone becomes the consum-
mate "fool" among the courtiers and noblemen. Of course, however,
only such a master dramatist as Shakespeare could devise such
magnificent "foolery."

Rosalind is imagined by those on stage to be summoned by the
magical enchantment of Hymen, and from her and Celia's entrances
on stage until the epilogue, the play becomes a fully realized masque. Short though it is however, this petite masque is the forerunner
of Shakespeare's grande masque in *The Tempest.*

Jaques is perhaps as consistent a character from beginning to
end as can be found in all of literature. For that reason, his exit is
wonderfully choice and witty; he who criticized country living from
the start, chooses to *remain* in the country, while all those from the
city or court, who extolled the virtues of pastoral life are now ready
to return to their former lives in the city. The fact that Jaques's

farewell is put in the form of a last will and testament is fitting because he will join Duke Frederick in a religious life, becoming, as it were, "dead" to the world. Yet in no sense will the memory of the mercurial Jaques be "dead"; his melodramatic posing, his "operatic" melancholy, and his realization that life itself is probably no more than a theatrical spectacle – all these qualities immortalize Jaques, the quintessence of "the man apart."

EPILOGUE

Summary

In keeping with the magical, dramatic effects of the last scene, Rosalind asks for the audience's approval by invoking some formulas of conjuration.

Commentary

"A good wine needs no bush," Rosalind's gay comment on the play, is a well-known proverb. The ivy bush was a well-known sign of the Elizabethan vintner, and the key to the humor here is to be found in Rosalind's, "If I were a woman . . . ." The role of Rosalind, remember, was always played by a beardless young chap.

CHARACTER ANALYSES

Orlando

Basically, Orlando de Boys is "everything that doth become a man" – that is, he epitomizes the Elizabethan concept of the ideal manly virtues, and he is also the embodiment of his late father's moral precepts. When the play begins, we hear him speaking about his late father's final wishes, and we realize the extent that Orlando's brother, Oliver de Boys, has violated those wishes. Thus the plot is begun and before the scene ends, the brothers almost come to physical blows when Oliver suggests that their father sired a "villain" in the person of Orlando.

Later in the play, Orlando is faced with the dilemma of whether or not he should let his evil brother be killed by a lioness or whether he (Orlando) should act according to the high moral standards of his father's precepts and save his brother's life. He reveals his disgust with evil when he begins to turn away from his brother's peril, but he evinces his moral worth finally when he decides to kill the lioness. Thus he becomes even more heroic than he has seemed heretofore; he becomes a model of moral goodness.

"This excellent young man" is, by birth, a gentleman, the son of an illustrious knight, and, as noted, he is fiercely loyal to his father's memory. The plot turns on the fact that Orlando has received only the most rudimentary upbringing; despite this unfortunate turn of events, however, his honorable nature is unimpaired, and the nobility of character which he inherited from his father, like the handsome physical features which he also inherited from his father, emerge as standards by which the rest of the men in this comedy can be judged by. Even Oliver, Orlando's hostile brother, acknowledges Orlando's fine character and popularity: ". . . he's gentle; never school'd and yet learned. . . ." (I.i.172-77). Orlando's courtesy, which gains him admiration and affection everywhere, is especially demonstrated when he is introduced to aristocratic society in Act I, Scene 2. In addition, his gentleness is exemplified in his solicitude for his old and ailing servant, Adam, in the Forest of Arden in Act II, Scene 6, and also in his decision to ultimately forgive his brother for his previous tyranny. In triumphing over the very human temptation to abandon his spiteful, hateful brother, Orlando reveals striking proof of his unselfish, good nature.

To these virtues may be added Orlando's sturdy independence, which prompts him to rebel against his servitude (I.i.). In addition to his admirable independence, his remarkable courage is shown when he volunteers, against powerful odds, to enter the ring with the brutish Charles, Duke Frederick's professional wrestler; he refuses to be dissuaded from fighting Charles and, as a result, his physical strength is displayed for us in his quick defeat of the enormously powerful wrestler who has just defeated three challengers; later, of course, the narration of Orlando's successful combat with the lioness in Act IV, Scene 3 is further proof of his physical heroism.

Although Orlando is a man of action, one should note that he can appreciate Rosalind's wit; he has a superbly facile mind, and he can more than hold his own in his encounters with Jaques, a man of wise loquacity, or so he thinks (III.ii.268-312). Even Jaques admires Orlando's mind: "You have a nimble wit," Jaques admiringly notes.

All in all, Orlando embodies his age's Anglo-Saxon virtues of courtesy, gentleness, independence, courage, strength, and filial devotion; and having established Orlando as a knight-of-sorts, Shakespeare then reveals his human frailities – in particular, when Rosalind gives Orlando a necklace, his strength, courage, and all his manly virtues desert him, momentarily, and he is speechless (I.ii.260-62). In this encounter with Rosalind, he is "overthrown" by love, even though he was *not* overthrown earlier by Charles, the gigantic wrestler. After Orlando's decision to escape to safety in the Forest of Arden, we see him primarily in the role of a man who is, in Shakespeare's words, "love-shak'd." He pins verses on trees in the forest and carves Rosalind's name into the bark of trees. Continually dreaming of Rosalind, he lies underneath the trees, "stretch'd along [in Celia's words], like a wounded knight" (III.ii.253-54). Although Orlando has seen Rosalind only once and has no certainty that he will see her again, he never wavers in his "true faith" for her, and, initially, he has no wish to be cured of his "love-sickness" (III.ii.446). Thus is Orlando, the strutting, fiery, strong, and sensual male, brought to bay not by a ferocious foe but by the whim of Eros. He is manacled not by a ball and chain but by a simple chain, the necklace from a beautiful woman's neck. And all this is achieved within the framework of one of Shakespeare's most popular and merry comedies.

In Shakespeare's day, the ideal man was a lover, as well as a physical hero; he excelled in sports and in battle, and he also celebrated his beloved in verse. And important to this definition of the ideal man is the fact that the ideal Renaissance man need *not* be a good poet (proof of this is in Orlando's poetry). This, of course, makes him, and the comedy, all the more delightful and human; Orlando is one of Shakespeare's most "human" creations – that is, he has his moments of weakness, but in many ways, he lives up to all the sterling ideals which have been for centuries the strengths of English character and culture.

Rosalind

Just as Orlando, the hero of the play, exemplifies the best of the Anglo-Saxon and Elizabethan virtues of a man, Rosalind, the heroine of this comedy, exemplifies the best of virtues to be found in a Renaissance English woman. She is intelligent, witty, warm, strong of character, and she possesses an unshakable integrity. Yet, there is nothing overbearing or pedantic about her intelligence; she intimidates no one. As a result, she remains always gently and wittily human, whereas Orlando, at times, seems almost too intense in his quest to measure up to his father's precepts. Rosalind always seems to rise above the failings of fate by using her resourceful, realistic understanding, and she emerges as a human being who is to be admired. "The people praise her for her virtues," Le Beau informs us (I.ii.291); her goodness and especially her ability to calmly endure misfortune are confirmed by Duke Frederick (I.iii.79-84).

But Rosalind's patience is not without limits. She is no saint, and she can assert herself with an authority appropriate to her status as the daughter of a duke. Falsely charged with treason and condemned to exile, she is nevertheless secure in her integrity, and she is able to defend herself with courteous yet firm eloquence (I.iii.47-67).

Rosalind's exceptional mental gifts are most strikingly demonstrated during the bright flow of her conversation. She can seemingly be witty on all occasions, and her repartee is especially sparkling when she is alone with Celia, when she's drawing out the philosophical Touchstone, or when she is caricaturing Jaques, and it must also be admitted that she is particularly charming when she is lovingly teasing Orlando.

Rosalind is a discerning judge of character. Jaques, for all of his "Continental" pretensions, does not impress her at all; in contrast, she appreciates the wisdom, as well as the occasional witty foolishness of Touchstone — a wisdom which the clown is not always fully aware of. That is, being a fool, Touchstone cannot be aware, she thinks, of how profoundly true his statements are. "Thou speak'st wiser than thou art ware of," she says, in response to Touchstone's speech about his courting with a "peascod" (II.iv.57-58). With a many-sided intelligence that is verbal, practical, and imaginative, Rosalind outshines everyone else, male and female, in the play. Her bright humor and ready wit are so much in evidence that her deeper feelings are too often overlooked. At first, she is depressed about her father's being exiled, but then in a revealing passage, she promises to make a conscious effort to forget her sorrows and appear happy:

"From henceforth I will [be merry], coz, and devise sports" (I.ii.26-27). This is proof that her surface gaiety is not always to be taken at face value.

Rosalind falls in love with Orlando at first sight; this we have seen and discussed. Impulsively, she declares her feelings by giving him her necklace and confessing:

> Sir, you have wrestled well, and overthrown
> More than your enemies.
>
> (I.ii.266-67)

And later, she is rashly impatient for Celia to identify the forester who has been decking the trees with verses in praise of Rosalind; when she is told that it is Orlando, she questions her cousin breathlessly (III.ii.189-244) and becomes concerned about her appearance—forgetting momentarily that she is in disguise as a man and shouldn't worry about such things. This sudden weakness is humorous; yet it is very human and girlish, and it receives understanding sympathy from the audience.

Although Rosalind laughs at love in her later bantering with Orlando ("Love is merely a madness"), she assures him (III.ii.420) that her cynicism is not to be taken literally. Later, for example, she is anxious and depressed when Orlando is late for their meeting in Act III, Scene 4, to cure his love-sickness. "Never talk to me!" she pleads with Celia, "I will weep." Rosalind's commitment to Orlando is total. "O coz, coz, coz, my pretty little coz," she exclaims to Celia, "that thou didst know how many fathom deep I am in love. . . . My affection hath an unknown bottom. . . ." (IV.i.209-13).

On the other hand, Rosalind's relationship with her father presents a possible stumbling block to the modern reader's appreciation of her warmly emotional nature. She chooses, for example, to remain with Celia, rather than join Duke Senior in exile (I.i.110-18); this decision, however, could have been based on a decision to obey her father, who could hardly expect his daughter to withstand the ". . . churlish chiding of the winter's wind" in the Forest of Arden. Significantly, it is Celia, rather than Rosalind, who proposes that they go into the Forest of Arden to seek the Duke (I.iii.109), and Rosalind's agreement is partly explained by the fact that she has just given her heart to Orlando; he occupies her every thought. Such a state of affairs is entirely natural in a romantic play, and Rosalind's final reunion with her father, Duke Senior, is as affectionate as could be wished (V.iv.122-24).

Favored with youth, beauty, intelligence, wit, and depth of feeling, Rosalind is one of Shakespeare's most appealing creations. She has, indeed, been frequently regarded as the ideal romantic heroine — very warm and very human, and in any good production, she dominates the stage.

Celia

Celia is in some ways the mirror which Shakespeare holds up to the audience to show the depths of Rosalind's passions. For that reason, the fact that Celia in many ways resembles Rosalind is not surprising. The two girls have almost identical backgrounds. They are princesses, cousins, and inseparable companions, brought up together from their earliest childhoods. Like Rosalind, Celia is physically attractive, intelligent, and witty; also, like Rosalind, she has a bright sense of humor. Both girls embody the essences of the ideal heroine. Celia also shares with Rosalind a reflective turn of mind, which is seen in their discussion of Fortune and Nature (I.ii.34-59).

Celia is not, however, a carbon copy of Rosalind. Rather, she serves as a foil, a mirror, a young woman who brings out, by contrast, the distinctive qualities of the play's heroine. That she shares the same virtues with Rosalind raises her attractiveness, of course, in the mind of the audience.

Although Celia is quite able to hold her own in witty conversations with Rosalind and Touchstone, she is usually reserved in public situations; in the important scenes in which both girls are present, the scenes are dominated by Rosalind. In Act III, Scene 2, for example, Celia says nothing for almost two hundred lines. This is to be explained, in part, by the fact that Rosalind is Shakespeare's principal creation, and by the fact that throughout most of the play, Celia *is not* in love. In terms of stage decorum, it is necessary that Celia, or someone else, be on stage during the courtship scenes to lend a certain respectability and to keep the scenes from degenerating into burlesque. Thus, Celia acts more or less as a "chaperone" in the play. When at last she finally falls in love herself, Celia is won over immediately by Oliver; she never takes part, however, in *her* courtship as does Rosalind in her own spirited, frustrated, and protracted courtship. Humorously, Orlando is incredulous at Celia's capitulation to his brother's avowals of love. "Is't possible," he asks Oliver, "that on so little acquaintance you should like her . . . and, wooing, she should grant?" (V.ii.1-5).

Celia provides yet another function in this play which is often overlooked by many modern-day audiences. She serves to remind the audience that Rosalind is an actor – that is, she is a *boy* who is playing the role of a girl who, in disguise, is playing the role of a young man. There is much humor in Rosalind's masquerade as "Ganymede." The epilogue, in particular, which is part of the burlesque of the play, loses much of its humor unless the audience remembers that the actor playing Rosalind was a boy in the Elizabethan productions.

Celia's role, then, is ultimately subordinate to that of her friend, Rosalind; she has the dramatically somewhat thankless part of serving as a companion, rather than as emerging as a strong personality in her own right. Yet without Celia's acting as a kind of mirror to Rosalind, Rosalind's character would lose a great deal of its brilliance. Celia's friendship for Rosalind is perhaps the most striking feature of her personality. We first see her comforting Rosalind (I.ii.1-32), and later, when the tyrannical Duke Frederick vilifies Rosalind, Celia springs to her cousin's defense, absolutely unaffected by her father's unjust remarks which are calculated to arouse her envy and resentment (I.iii.68-88). It is Celia who proposes that the two young women flee the palace and run off together. Importantly, Celia does not once hesitate to leave the comforts of the court in order to face the dangers of exile in order to be with her friend. Denied great romantic scenes in the play, Celia nevertheless shines passionately as the devoted friend of Rosalind, loyal, precise, and ever practical.

Touchstone

In the stage directions of the First Folio, Touchstone is designated as being a "clowne"; later, he is referred to as a "fool." Basically, the term "clowne" was more applicable to a country bumpkin, whereas the term "fool" was applied to the professional jester – that is, the fool, the king's jester, dressed in motley. In reading Elizabethan plays, it is important to keep this important distinction in mind.

In Act I, Scene 2, Celia and Rosalind refer to Touchstone as a "natural." Here, Touchstone's character changes yet a bit more; Rosalind is saying that he is a born fool or idiot, but this is wholly out of keeping with what we know of Rosalind's character. Obviously, this is most likely a pun on the words "natural" and "nature," words which occur frequently in the scene. The comic banter of the two girls here is used as a contrast to the somber opening scene, and it is also used to establish the comic device of the pun, a word play which Elizabethan audiences never tired of. The extended pun on "natural" and "nature" in this scene where Touchstone's "wisdom" is questioned, culminates in Celia's remark, "the dullness of the fool is the whetstone of the wits" (I.ii.58-59).

Touchstone, more appropriately, is described by Jaques as being "a motley fool" (II.vii.13). Here, Jaques is describing the professional jester, easily recognized by his costume, which was usually a child's long coat, gathered at the waist and falling in folds below the knees. A bauble was sometimes worn on the sleeve, and a cockscomb or feather decorated the hat.

Whatever the case in this particular scene, Touchstone's motley is sober enough to entitle him to treatment as a gentleman in the Forest of Arden. As a matter of fact, Touchstone fancies himself a courtier, and Jaques reports on Touchstone's pretensions of being a courtier in Act II, Scene 7, lines 36-38, and again when he introduces the fool to Duke Senior:

> *Jaq.* He hath been a courtier, he swears.
> *Touch.* If any man doubt that, let him put me to my
> purgation. I have trod a measure; I have flatt'red a lady
> . . . I have undone three tailors; I have had four quarrels,
> and like to have fought one.
>
> (V.iv.42-49)

Touchstone has also assumed the role of a courtier in his meeting with Corin. Personally, he feels far superior to the pastoral shepherd; his criticism of pastoral life proceeds from his assumption of the superiority of sophisticated court life over country living.

Later, Touchstone burlesques the artificiality of the gentlemanly code of honor (V.iv.48-108), which is in keeping, of course, with his multifaceted personality.

Another interesting aspect of Touchstone's character is the fact that he is restricted in his singing. Shakespeare usually gives some songs to his fools. Yet here, Touchstone sings only snatches of song. Several explanations have been advanced as to why Touchstone is not given more songs to sing, but all arguments remain only conjectures.

Finally, it must be acknowledged that in a fantasy such as *As You Like It*, it is not necessary that every character be fully developed. The strength of this play lies in its dialogue and in its masque-like elements. That Touchstone is not truly and fully developed as a character does not detract from the play. That he is a superb example of theatrical convention is enough, and in no way does it detract from his effectiveness as an integral part of the play. His wit is the wit of a master dramatist, even if he remains, ultimately, incomplete, an enigma of contradictions.

CRITICAL ANALYSIS

The Natural and the Artificial

Shakespeare's themes are often expressed in terms of oppositions, such as the conflicting values associated with fair and foul in *Macbeth. As You Like It* is no exception. Running throughout *As You Like It* is a tension of antithesis between the natural (that which is free, spontaneous, and wholesome) and the artificial (that which is constrained, calculated, and unnatural). The clash between these two ways of life is seen on several levels: (1) social: in the values associated with civilized society (the court or a great country estate) compared with the value of simple living (the open pastures and the forest encampment); (2) familial: in the strife that sets brother against brother and parent against child; and (3) personal: in the contrast between courtships which are based upon genuine emotion (Orlando and Rosalind) and those which are based on formal conventions (Silvius and Phebe). These various levels are not kept distinct in the play, however, and disorder in one area is likely to parallel disorder in another.

The first scene of the play introduces us to organized life on a country estate. Here the close ties which should unite brothers have been perverted. The unnaturalness of the situation is made clear in Orlando's opening speech. He has been kept from his modest patrimony, his gentle birth has been undermined, and he speaks of "mutiny" and "servitude." Oliver's brutal treatment of the faithful servant Adam, whom he addresses as an "old dog," shows that the disorder affects other members of the household as well. In the same scene we learn of an earlier, parallel perversion of normal family life, but here the roles are reversed, with the young men's father, a *younger* brother abusing his *older* brother. The wrestler, Charles, reports that "the old Duke is banished by his younger brother, the new Duke." On the social level, the corruption of the great estate is matched by the debasement of court life.

But in opposition to these sinister currents, we witness a strong element of harmony between relations: Celia loves her cousin Rosalind so much that she will follow her into exile or else stay behind with her and die. And we learn too of a harmonious social order established by the banished Duke Senior and his "merry men" in the Forest of Arden. Thus the opposition between court and country, the natural and the artificial, is established at the outset of the play.

In Act I, Scene 2, the corruptions of court life are overtly shown; there is little subtlety here. For example, the clown speaks jestingly of a knight without honor who has nevertheless prospered under Frederick, the reigning duke. Not long afterwards, Orlando, who has just won the wrestling match, is denied the honor due him for his triumph because his father, whom "the world esteem'd . . . honourable," was the usurper's enemy. The natural values subverted in the earlier scenes find glowing representation in Act II, Scene 1 – that is, "painted pomp," "the envious court," and "public haunt" give way to the uncomplicated rewards of a life close to trees and running brooks. Here, the banished Duke Senior and his "co-mates and brothers in exile" find their existence "sweet." But to achieve full contentment they have had to adjust themselves to the natural hardships of their lot – "the icy fang/ And churlish chiding of the winter's wind."

The pattern of accommodation is one which the various fugitives in the Forest of Arden go through; to them, the forest at first appears wild rather than green, and threatening rather than hospitable. Rosalind complains that her spirits are weary; Celia is too exhausted to continue; Touchstone frankly declares, "When I was at home, I was in a better place." Orlando and Adam almost starve, and Orlando speaks of the "uncouth [rough] forest," "the bleak air," and "this desert." Oliver becomes a "wretched ragged man" threatened by savage beasts.

But all of these characters eventually make their peace with the forest, and even the tyrant, Duke Frederick, is converted when he comes "to the skirts of this wild." For Orlando, the reconciliation is effected when he, along with Adam, joins Duke Senior's feast. The grand movement of the play, then is from organized society to the country, from constraint to freedom, and from hardship to joy. "Now go we in content," Celia says on the eve of her exile, "to liberty, and not to banishment."

Shakespeare's Forest of Arden furnishes the setting against which most of the action unfolds, but it serves as much more than a mere backdrop. The greenwood assumes symbolic stature. First of all, it is 1) an "idyllic forest." The words used by Charles to describe Duke Senior's life in the forest suggest an idyllic existence, and in the famous pastoral romances of Shakespeare's day, a world is created in which shepherds and shepherdesses sing, pipe tunes, and make love while their flocks graze carelessly in green valleys bright with the sunshine of eternal summer. This golden world, needless to say, has little relation to the actualities of country living in any age; yet it is the artist's fulfillment of the universal longing to flee burdensome realities and find quietude and peace. In Shakespeare's time, no less than in ours, people felt the need for just such an escape. This idyllic concept of Arden is introduced, as was noted, by the rumor reported by Charles in the first scene, and to this Forest of Arden (a name that has since become synonymous with a forest utopia) belong such creatures as Silvius and Phebe, whose names and behavior link them to later Acadian literature. These characters are absorbed entirely in the sighing disquietudes of love, as only the shepherds and shepherdesses of romance can afford to do.

The greenwood of Arden is also, of course, symbolic of 2) an "actual forest." Shakespeare's Forest of Arden is subject to the changes wrought by the seasons, and even the stoic Duke Senior admits finally that he and his company have suffered "shrewd days and nights."

Furthermore, the presence of Touchstone and Jaques in the forest provides what one critic has called "counterstatements" to the theme of rural contentment. To Jaques, the exchange of civilized comfort for country hardships is symptomatic of human stubbornness, as his contemptuous parody of "under the greenwood tree" makes evident (II.v.52-59). Touchstone, on the other hand, is an example of Shakespeare's sense of irony about pastoral joys, for he plays the role of a discontented exile from the court. Under the guise of apparent nonsense (in his reply to Corin's query about how he likes the shepherd's life (III.ii.12-22), Touchstone mocks the contradictory nature of the desires ideally resolved by pastoral life – that is, to be at the same time at court and in the fields and to enjoy both the advantages of rank, in addition to the advantages of the classless estate of Arden. This sort of humor goes to the heart of the pastoral convention and shows how very clearly Shakespeare understood it and could use it to its best, humorous advantage.

The realities of country living are squarely faced in the characters of Audrey, who is no beauteous damsel; William, who is no poetical swain; and Corin, who is a simple "true labourer" in the pastures. If Silvius and Phebe find their places in Shakespeare's complex Arden, their romancing is presented as frankly *artificial*, in contrast with both the elemental, biological basis of Touchstone's pursuit of Audrey and the profoundly felt love experienced by Rosalind and Orlando. Thus, Silvius and Phebe, pastoral stereotypes, provide another instance of the opposition between the natural and the unnatural, which is always a dominant thematic concern of the play.

QUESTIONS FOR REVIEW

1. List the "town" characters in the play, enumerate their attributes, and discuss how they reflect town life. Use the same format for the "country" characters.

2. There are four pairs of lovers in the play. Characterize each couple and discuss the concept of love which they represent.

3. Give several examples showing how Shakespeare uses language to indicate class differences among the characters.

4. There are many words in the play that have changed in their meanings since Shakespeare's time. Make a list of those significant words which are germane to a thorough understanding the play. Discuss how only a present-day meaning of the words can bring about a misunderstanding of the play.

5. What purpose does Rosalind's disguise serve in the play?

6. Discuss the advantages of "town life" over that of "country life." Reverse the situation. How does Shakespeare resolve this debate?

7. Of different types of love shown in the play, which does Shakespeare seem to favor? In which characters does this evince itself and to what extent?

8. Discuss the various types of humor in the play. Compare or contrast the wit of Touchstone with that of Jaques; with Corin; and with Rosalind.

9. Why is it necessary for the main characters to meet climactically in the Forest of Arden?

10. The Forest of Arden has been said to be, in actuality, the Forest of the Ardennes on the Meuse River in Europe. Yet, there is a Forest of Arden in England. Where do you think it is located? Why?

11. List the masque-like elements in the play.

12. What stage conventions were popular with Elizabethan audiences? Give specific references from the play to support your answers.

13. What use does Shakespeare make of shifting his scenes—that is, from a courtly scene to a pastoral scene, etc.?

14. Where is the dramatic climax in the play? Where is the literary climax in the play?

15. How do the characters reflect the time in which Shakespeare wrote?

SELECTED BIBLIOGRAPHY

ADAMS, J. Q. *A Life of William Shakespeare*. Boston: Houghton Mifflin Co., 1923.

ALEXANDER, PETER. *Shakespeare*. Oxford: Oxford University Press, 1964.

BEVINGTON, DAVID. *Shakespeare*. Arlington Heights, Ill,: A.H.M. Publications, 1978.

BLOOM, EDWARD A., ed. *Shakespeare 1564-1964*. Providence: Brown University Press, 1964.

FARNHAM, WILLARD. *The Medieval Heritage of Elizabethan Tragedy*. Berkeley, California: University of California Press, 1936.

GIBSON, H. N. *The Shakespeare Claimants*. New York: Barnes & Noble, Inc., 1962.

HEILMAN, ROBERT B. *Magic in the Web*. Lexington, Kentucky: University of Kentucky Press, 1956.

HAYLES, N. K. "Sexual Disguise in *As You Like It* and *Twelfth Night, Shakespeare Survey*, Vol. 32, pp. 63-72, 1978.

HIBBARD, G. R. "Love, Marriage and Money in Shakespeare's Theatre and Shakespeare's England," *The Elizabethan Theatre*, Vol. 7, pp. 134-55, 1979.

KANTAK, V. Y. "An Approach to Shakespearean Comedy," *Shakespeare Survey*, Vol. 22, pp. 7-14, 1974.

KNIGHT, G. WILSON. *The Wheel of Fire.* London: Oxford University Press, 1930.

LEAVIS, F. R. *The Common Pursuit.* Hardmonsworth, Middlesex: Penguin Books, Ltd., 1963.

LERNER L. *The Uses of Nostalgia.* Schocken, 1972.

SEWELL, ARTHUR. *Character and Society in Shakespeare.* Oxford: Clarendon Press, 1951.

SMITH, JAMES. *Shakespearean and Other Essays*, Cambridge, 1974.

WEISS, T. "Breath of Clowns and Kings," *Nation*, Aug. 16, 1971.

NOTES

NOTES

NOTES

NOTES

NOTES